$1

THE LESSON OF LIFE

THE LESSON OF LIFE

178 Sayings
in the Handwriting of
THE MOTHER

Sri Aurobindo Ashram
Pondicherry, India

First edition 1984
Fifth impression 2013

Rs 120
ISBN 978-81-7058-474-2

© Sri Aurobindo Ashram Trust 1984
Published by Sri Aurobindo Ashram Publication Department
Pondicherry 605 002
Web http://www.sabda.in

Printed at Sri Aurobindo Ashram Press, Pondicherry
PRINTED IN INDIA

Publisher's Note

This book contains facsimiles of 178 sayings chosen by the Mother and written in her hand. Thirty-seven of them are words of her own, mainly sentences from her *Prayers and Meditations*. Twenty-three are statements taken from the writings of Sri Aurobindo. The remaining 118 were gleaned from the world's scriptures and from the works of various thinkers and sages of the East and West. The first entry in the book is Sri Aurobindo's neatly penned transcription of a letter first written on an earlier occasion.

The genesis of the book is this: In the autumn of 1934, a young man asked the Mother if she would write one sentence a day to him. When she agreed to do so, he presented her with a bound notebook in which to write. By filling up one page a day, the Mother completed the notebook in the course of six months. That handwritten book is now – fifty years later – being reproduced for a wider audience.

It is the lesson of life that always in this world everything fails a man — only the Divine does not fail him, if he turns entirely to the Divine. It is not because there is something bad in you that blows fall on you; — blows fall on all human beings because they are full of desire for things that cannot last and they lose them or, even if they get, it brings disappointment and cannot satisfy them. To turn to the Divine is the only truth in life.

Sri Aurobindo

21·4·33

2. 11. 34.

The Buddha has said:

"There is more joy in
one desire conquered than
in a thousand desires
satisfied."

3-11. 34.

Saadi, the Persian poet,
has said:

"Contemplate the mirror
of thy heart and thou
shalt taste little by little
a pure joy and unmixed
peace."

4-11-34.

Another Buddhist saying:

"The mind constructs its
own abode; directed falsely from
the beginning it thinks in
erroneous ways and engenders
its own distress. Thought
creates for itself its own
suffering."

6.11.34.

The Buddhist Scriptures from
the Chinese, tell us:

"Let us watch over our thoughts."

"A bad thought is the most
dangerous of thieves."

7 - 11 - 34.

The Mahayana teaches thus:

"When the disciple considering an idea sees rise in him bad or unhealthy thoughts, thoughts of covetousness, hatred or error, he should either turn his mind away from that idea, or concentrate it upon a healthy thought, or else examine the fatal nature of the idea, or analyse it and decompose it into its different elements, or, making appeal to all his strength and applying the greatest energy, suppress it from his mind; thus are removed and disappear these bad and unhealthy ideas and the mind becomes firm, calm unified full of vigour."

8 - 11 - 34.

Angelus Silesius, the Christian
mystic, has said:

"Eternal wisdom builds:
I shall be her palace when
she finds repose in me and
I in her."

9-11-34.

The following saying can be
read in the Book of Wisdom:

"We fight to win sublime
Wisdom; therefore men call us
warriors."

10.11.34.

Ramakrishna very wisely said.

"Whoever thinks himself an
imperfect and worldly soul,
is really an imperfect and
worldly soul; whoever deems
himself divine, becomes
divine. What a man
thinks he is, he becomes."

11 - 11 - 34.

Seneca has said.

" Let us lend ear to the
sages who point out to us the
way. "

12 - 11 - 34 .

In the Proverbs we read:

" He that walketh with
the wise, shall be wise . "

13 - 11 - 34 .

The Mahaparinibhana Sutta
teaches thus :

" To avoid the company of
fools, to be in communion with
the sages, to render honour to
that which merits honour, is
a great blessedness."

14-11-34.

Here is on of Ramakrishna's sayings:

" The company of saints and sages is one of the chief agents of spiritual progress."

15 - 11 - 34.

The ancient wisdom of China says:

" He who knows how to find instructors for himself, arrives at the supreme mastery .....
He who loves to ask, extends his knowledge; but whoever considers only his own personal opinion becomes constantly narrower than he was. "

16 . 11 . 34

The Epistle to the Hebrews gives
this advice:

"Obey them that guide you
and submit yourselves; for they
watch over your souls."

17-11-34.

Saint Paul says in the first Epistle
to the Thessalonians:

"And we beseech you to
know Them who labour among
you and are over you and
admonish you and to
esteem them very highly in
love for their work's sake."

18 - 11 - 34.

Confucius has said:

" It is impossible to arrive
at the summit of the
mountain without passing
through rough and difficult
paths. "

19-4-34.

In the Bhagavad Gita one reads:

"All that man does comes to its perfection in knowledge. That do thou learn by prostration to the wise and by questioning and by serving them; they who have the knowledge and see the truths of things shall instruct thee in the knowledge."

20 - 11 - 34

In very ancient Egypt
Ptah - Hotep said:

"Do what thy Master
tells thee; it is good."

21 - 11 - 34.

Here is another good advice from
Ramakrishna:

"Do not listen if one criticises
or blames thy Master, leave
his presence that very moment."

22 - 11 - 34.

Another saying of
Ramakrishna :

" One who thinks that his
spiritual guide is merely a
man, can draw no profit
from his contact. "

23 - 11 - 34.

The great Egyptian initiate
Hermes has said:

"Things mortal change their
aspect daily; they are nothing
but a lie."

24 - 11 - 34 .

Giordano Bruno has said:

" The external forms are alone
subject to change and destruction;
for these forms are not the
things themselves. Deliver thyself
from the inconstancy of .
human things."

27 -11. 34.

In the Book of Knowledge one can read:

"When thou hast recognised the impermanence of all formations, thou shalt contemplate that which does not perish and remains for ever."

28 - 11 - 34.

The Book of Golden Precepts
tells us:

" Silence thy thoughts and fix
all thy attention on the Master within
whom thou seest not yet, but
of whom thou hast a presentiment."

29.11.34.

Baha'Ullah has said:

"The seeker ought to avoid any preference of himself to another; he should efface pride and arrogance from his heart, arm himself with patience and endurance and follow the law of silence so that he may keep himself from vain words."

Yn

30 - 11 - 34.

Here is a saying from Hermes:

"The eyes of our mentality are
incapable as yet of contemplating
the incorruptible and incomprehensible
Beauty.... Thou shalt see it
when thou hast nothing to say
concerning it; for knowledge,
for contemplation are silence,
are the sinking to rest of all
sensation.".

1-12, 34.

Emerson has said:

"It is God within who pushes the tongue of prayer by a sublimer thought. A voice speaks to us in the depths of the heart, "I am, my child, and by me are and subsist thy body and the luminous world. I am, all things are in me and all that is mine is thine."

2-12-34

Here is what Carlyle says
about silence:

" When one considers the
clamorous emptiness of the world,
words of so little sense, actions
of so little merit, one loves to
reflect on the great reign of
silence. The noble silent men
scattered here and there each in
his province silently thinking
and silently acting, of whom
no morning paper makes
mention, these are the salt
of the earth."

3.12.34.

and this is from Emerson:

"Real action is done in moments
of silence."

4 - 12. 34

In the Book of Golden
Precepts we read this:

" Before the soul can understand
and remember it must be
united to Him who speaks
by His silence, as to the mind
of the potter the form on which
the clay is modelled. "

5. 12. 34.

An advice from the Orphic Hymns:

"Love light and not darkness."

6 - 12. 34.

Here is a bit of Chinese
wisdom expressed by
Meng-Tse :

" Our inner self is provided
with all necessary faculties."

7-12.34.

Ramakrishna has said:

"If you live one sixteenth part
of what I teach you, you will
attain the goal"

8 - 12 . 34 .

Confucius has said:

"There is as much virtue
in the humblest things as in
the most sublime."

(signature)

9-12-34.

One can read in the Chu-king:

" It is easy to know what is good,
but not so easy to practice it. "

                                    [signature]

10 - 12 - 34

Demophilus has said:

"Do what thou knowest to be good without expecting from it any glory. Forget not that the Vulgar are a bad judge of good actions."

11 . 12 . 34

Antoine the Healer has said:

"Often man is preoccupied with
human rules and forgets the
inner law."

12 . 12 . 34 .

We read in the Sutra in 42 articles :

" The important thing is to
practise what is taught. It is no
use being with the Master if one
does not oneself practise or
cannot profit by it. "

yi

13.12.34.

Confucius has said:

" It is better to love the Truth than
merely to know its principles, but
better than loving the Truth is to
make it one's sole delight and
practice. "

14 - 12 - 34.

In the Zendavesta we read:

" Let this be thy aim to have
always the right thought, right
speech, right action."

15 - 12 - 34.

Baha-Ullah has said:

"In the world of unity heaven and earth are one".

16 . 12 . 34 .

The Book of Golden Precepts
teaches:

"One must learn to dissipate
the shadow and live in that which
is eternal . For that you must
live and breathe in all as all
you perceive lives in you ; you
must feel that you are in
all things and all things
in yourself . "

Mira

17 - 12 - 34.

Hermes has said:

"Raise thyself above every height, descend below every depth, assemble in thyself all the sensations of created things, of water, of fire, of the dry, of the moist; suppose that thou art at once every-where, on earth, in the sea, in the heavens, that thou wast never born, that thou art still in the womb, that thou art young, old, dead, beyond death; comprehend all at once, times, spaces, things, qualities, and thou shalt comprehend God."

18.12.34

and again Hermes has said:

" Surpass all bodies, traverse
all times, become eternity and
thou shalt comprehend God. "

mji ———————

19. 12. 34

The buddhist scripture Fo-sho-hing-Tsan-king
tells us:

"When you have learned the
teaching, let your purified hearts
find their joy in doing actions
that are in harmony with it."

20-12-34.

Schopenhauer has said:

"It is one and the same
Being who manifests in all
that lives."

21 . 12 . 34 .

Sri Aurobindo says :

" There is no greater pride and
glory than to be a perfect instrument
of the Master."

22. 12. 34.

Sri Aurobindo says:

"Be conscious first of
thyself within, then think
and act."

23.12.34.

Sri Aurobindo says :

"Immortality, unity and freedom
are in ourselves and await there
our discovery; but for the joy of
love God in us will still remain
the Many."

24 . 12 - 34 .

Sri Aurobindo says:

"Those who are poor, ignorant,
ill-born or ill-bred are not the
common herd; the common herd
are all who are satisfied with
pettiness and an average
humanity."

25-12-34.

Sri. Aurobindo says:

"Love is the keynote, Joy is the music, Power is the strain, Knowledge is the performer, the infinite All is the composer and audience. We know only the preliminary discords which are as fierce as the harmony shall be great; but we shall arrive surely at the fugue of the divine Beatitudes."

26.12.34.

Sri Aurobindo says:

"What I cannot do now is the sign of what I shall do hereafter. The sense of impossibility is the beginning of all possibilities."

27.12.34.

Sri Aurobindo says:

" There is no more benumbing error than to mistake a stage for the goal or to linger too long in a resting-place."

28 - 12 - 34.

Sri Aurobindo says:

" Patience is our first great necessary lesson, but not the dull slowness to move of the timid, the sceptical, the weary, the slothful, the unambitious or the weakling; a patience full of a calm and gathering strength which watches and prepares itself for the hour of swift great strokes, few but enough to change destiny. "

29-12-34.

Sri Aurobindo says:

   "God has all time before him
and does not need to be
always in a hurry."

30 - 12 . 34.

Sri Aurobindo says:

" Immortality, unity and freedom are in ourselves and await there our discovery."

31 - 12 - 34.

Sri Aurobindo says:

"In all these things there is a meaning and for all these contradictions there is a release."

1 - 1. 35.

Prayer of the 31st December
midnight :

"We surrender up to Thee,
this evening, all that is artificial
and false, all that pretends and
imitates. Let is disappear with
the year that is at an end.
May only what is perfectly true,
sincere, straight and pure
subsist in the year that is
beginning."

2.1.35 -

Mohy-ud'Din-arabi has said:

" When one discovers the enigma
of a single atom, one can see
the mystery of all creation, that
within us as well as that without. "

3 - 1 - 3 5.

Sri Aurobindo says:

"When we have passed beyond enjoyings, then we shall have Bliss. Desire was the helper; desire is the bar."

4.1.35

Sri Aurobindo says:

"When we have passed beyond
individualising, then we shall be
real Persons. Ego was the helper;
ego is the bar."

5 - 1. 35.

Sri Aurobindo says:

" All would change if man
could once consent to be
spiritualised. "

6 . 1 . 35

Sri Aurobindo says :

" The Spirit is the truth of our being;
mind and life and body in their
imperfection are its masks, but
in their perfection should be its
moulds. "

7 - 1 - 35.

Sri Aurobindo says :

"All religions have saved a
number of souls, but none yet
has been able to spiritualise
mankind."

8-1.35

Sri Aurobindo says:

"Distrust a perfect-seeming success,
but when having succeeded thou
findest still much to do, rejoice
and go forward; for the labour
is long before the real perfection."

9 . 1 . 35

Lao Tse has said:

" When the intelligence is master
over the vital movements, then
one has force. "

10 - 1 - 35.

Manu has said:

" One should destroy through deep meditation the qualities that are contrary to the divine nature. "

11 - 1 . 35

Lao Tse has said:

" The spiritual man thinks
more of what is within him
than of outer things. "

12 - 1 - 35

Lao Tze has said also:

"He makes his thought dynamic,
he opens his heart, he assembles the
inner lights."

13 . 1 . 35

We read in the Dhammapada:

"Thought is difficult to controle, light, running where it will; to master it is very helpful; for, mattered, it brings happiness."

14 . 1 - 35

again we find in the Dhammapada:
"As in a house with a good roof
the rain cannot penetrate, so
into the concentrated mind
passion cannot enter."

15.1.35.

Patanjali has said:

"When concentration becomes
natural and easy, a power
of accurate discrimination
begins to develop."

16.1.35.

We read in the Upanishad:

"The mind and senses are like a chariot drawn by wild horses, the wise man is careful to keep them well under rein."

17 - 1 - 35.

We read in the Book of Golden
Precepts :

" Be master of thy thoughts
O thou who strivest after perfection."

18 - 1 - 35 .

In the Imitation of Christ it is said:

"How can a man remain at peace
who is busy with alien cares, tries
to spread himself outside and
withdraws within very little
or rarely."

19 - 1. 35

Bahá-Ulláh has said:

"He shall pass from doubt
to certitude, from the darkness
of error to the light of the
Guidance; he shall see with
the eye of knowledge and
begin to commune in secret
with the Well - Beloved."

20.1.35

Giordano Bruno has said:

"Those who follow carefully the
inner contemplation have no
grief to fear; no vicissitude of
fate can touch them. They observe
the history written within to guide
them in the execution of the
divine laws which also are
engraved within in our hearts."

21 - 1 - 35.

Ramakrishna has said:

"Let not thoughts and anxieties trouble your mind. Do all that is necessary at its proper time, but let your mind be always fixed on the Divine."

22.1.35.

Sri Aurobindo says:

"The Divine gives itself to those
who give themselves without
reserve and in all their parts to
the Divine. For them the calm,
the light, the power, the bliss, the
freedom, the wideness, the heights
of knowledge, the seas of Ananda."

23 . 1 - 35.

Ramakrishna has said:

"The greater the aspiration
and concentration, the more
one finds the Eternal."

24 . 1 . 35

"If we go a little way within ourselves, we shall discover that there is in each of us a consciousness that has been living throughout the ages and manifesting in a multitude of forms."

25 - 1 - 35.

Ramakrishna has said:

" When a man is able to
concentrate his mind, then wherever
he may be he can always rise
above his surroundings and
rest in the Eternal ".

26.1.35.

" When you sit in meditation you
must be as candid and simple
as a child, not interfering by
your external mind, expecting
nothing, insisting on nothing.
Once this condition is there, all
the rest depends upon the aspiration
deep within you." .... "And
if you call upon Divinity, then
too ..... you will have the
answer."

27 . 1 . 35 .

Ramakrishna has said:

"It is an old saying 'Whoever is perfect in meditation is near to liberation'. Do you know when a man is perfect in meditation? When as soon as he sits to meditate the atmosphere of the Divine is around him and his soul is in touch with the Ineffable."

28.1.35

Sri Aurobindo says:

" In the end a union, a closeness,
a constant companionship
in the soul with the Divine,
and a yet more wonderful
oneness and in living. "

29.1.35.

" One Divine Consciousness
is here working through all
these beings, preparing its way
through all these manifestations.
At this day it is here at
work upon earth more
powerfully than it has
ever been before. "

30.1.35

Minokhired has said:

"Wisdom is a thing of which one can never have enough."

1 - 2 - 35.

Job has said:

"To have wisdom is worth
more than pearls."

2 . 2 . 35 .

Porphyry has said :

"The possession of wisdom
leadeth to true happiness."

J.K.

3 - 2 - 35

Theng - Tse has said:

"In this state of pure
felicity the soul is enlarged
and the material substance
that is subject to it profiteth
also."

4-2-35.

The Ecclesiasticus says:

" Wisdom strengtheneth the wise
more than ten mighty men which
are in a city."

5 . 2 . 35

Porphyry has said:

"To find our real being and know it truly is to acquire wisdom."

6 - 2 - 35.

"See how outer circumstances
are of little importance ... Be
more supple, more trusting ....
It is in the Calm of the deep waters
that is found the only possibility
of true Service."

"Torment thyself not, child,
silence, peace, peace."
(August 1913)

7 - 2 - 35

The Book of Wisdom says:

"Having thought of these things,
meditating on them in my heart and
having considered that I shall
find immortality in the union
with Wisdom, I went in search
of her on all sides, that I
might take her for my companion."

8 . 2 . 35.

a prayer -

" May all escape from the
ordinary consciousness and
be delivered from the attachment
for material things; may they
awake to the knowledge of Thy
divine Presence, unite themselves
with Thy supreme Consciousness.
and taste the plenitude of Peace
that springs from it."
(February 1914.)

9 - 2 - 35

The book of Wisdom says:

"I have preferred wisdom
to kingdoms and thrones and
I have believed that riches
are nothing before Wisdom,
for she is an endless treasure
for men."

10 - 2 . 35

Here is a Formula of devotion of
Mahayanist Buddhism :

" Honour to the high and sublime
excellence of Wisdom ! "

11 - 2 - 35

"In the calm contemplation
that precedes the dawn, better
than at any other moment,
my thought rises to Thee, O Lord
of our being, in an ardent prayer:
may this day which is about
to begin bring to the earth a
little more pure light and
true peace."

12 - 2 - 35

The Lalita Vistara says:

"That which satisfies the soul is the Wisdom which governs the world."

13 . 2 . 35.

In the Buddhist Meditations
from the Japanese we read:

"Wisdom is like unto a
beacon set on high, which
radiates its light even in
the darkest night."

14.2.35

The Fo-shu-hing-tsan-king says:

"As the light of a torch illumines the objects in a dark room, even so the light of wisdom illumines all men, whosoever they be, if they turn towards it."

9-3-32

Greed, greed, always greed ... is the response of material nature.

In whatever way the Divine manifests there, it becomes at once an object of covetousness. A rush to appropriate, an endeavour to rob, exploit, squeeze, swallow and, in the end, crush down the Divine, this is the receptivity of matter to the divine touch ...

O my Lord, Thou comest as the Redeemer and these would make of Thee a dupe! Thou comest for union, for transformation, for Realisation, and they think only of absorption and selfish increase ...

14 - 12 - 32 -

If it is the Will of the Supreme
that those who depend on me
should have no faith in me,
I have nothing to say. I am
responsible only for the
absoluteness of my own sincerity.

15 - 2 . 35 .

(a prayer)

"O Thou, inconceivable splendour,
O Thou, conqueror of all ignorance,
vanquisher of all egoism, Thou
who dost illumine hearts and
enlighten minds, Thou who art
Knowledge, Love and Existence,
let me live constantly in the
consciousness of Thy Unity, let
me ever conform to Thy Will."

16 . 2 . 35 .

The Book of Wisdom says:

" The desire for wisdom leads us
to the Eternal Kingdom."

17 . 2 . 35

Again the Book of Wisdom
says :

" Wisdom is full of light
and her beauty is not
withered . "

18 . 2 . 35 .

" Spiritual experience means the
contact with the Divine in oneself
(or without, which comes to the same
thing in that Domain). And it is an
experience identical everywhere in
all countries, among all peoples and
even in all ages."

19 - 2 - 35.

It is said in the Ecclesiasticus:

" I am the Mother of pure love
and of science and of sacred
hope. "

20 - 2.35 -

a prayer :

" Let me live constantly in Thy
Divine Love, so that it may
live in me and through me. "

21 - 2 - 35.

a prayer :

"O Lord, our heart is light,
our thought at rest. We turn
to Thee with full trust and
say peacefully :
May Thy will be done, in it
is realised true harmony.

22.2.35.

The Book of Wisdom says:

"I have learnt all that was hidden
and all that was yet undiscovered
because I was taught by Wisdom
herself that created everything."

23 - 2 - 35.

Angelus Silesius has said:

"Eternal Wisdom builds:
I shall be her palace when
she finds repose in me and
I in her."

24.2.35.

It is said in the Buddhist Canons in Pali:

"True knowledge does not grow old, so have declared the sages of all times."

25.2.35.

In the Inscriptions of Asoka
one can read:

"May the partisans of all
doctrines in all countries unite
and live in a common fellowship.
For all alike profess mastery
to be attained over oneself
and purity of the heart."

26 . 2 . 35 .

(meditation)

"Blessed be the day when I came to know Thee, O Ineffable Eternity!

Blessed among all days be that day when the earth at last awakened shall know Thee and shall live for Thee!"

27 - 2 . 35 .

St Luke has said:

"The dayspring from on high has
visited us . to give light to them
that sit in the darkness and in
the shadow of death, to guide
our feet in the way of peace."

28.2.35.

Hermes has said:

" Language is different but man is the same everywhere."

1 - 3 . 35.

(Meditation)

"O my divine Master, Thou hast
taken my life and made it Thine;
Thou hast taken my love and
identified it with Thine; Thou
hast taken my thought and
replaced it by Thy absolute
consciousness."

2 . 3 . 35

Tsen-tse has said:

"The sage's rule of moral conduct
has its principle in the hearts
of all men."

3.3.35

(a prayer)

"Deliver us, O Lord, from obscurity;
grant that we may become
perfectly awakened...."

4.3.35.

Tolstoi has said:

"In order to live a happy life, man
should understand what life is and
what he can or cannot do."

5 - 3 - 35

(a prayer)

"O sweet Master of love, grant
that my whole conciousness
be concentrated in Thee so that
I may live only by love and
light, and that love and
light may radiate through me
and awaken in all upon
the way."

6.3.35.

(Meditation)

"At each moment all the unforeseen, the unexpected, the unknown is before us, at each moment the universe creates itself anew in its entirety and in every one of its parts."

7 . 3 . 35

Schopenhauer has said:

" Will is the soul of the universe."

8 - 3 - 35

Sri Aurobindo says

" There is no stage of the sadhana
in which works are impossible,
no passage in the path where there
is no foothold and action has to be
renounced as incompatible with
concentration on the Divine."

9 - 3 - 35.

Hermes has said:

"Each separate movement is
produced by the same energy
that moves the sum of things."

10 - 3 - 35.

(meditation)

"O Lord, the hour of Thy manifestation
has come and soon canticles of
rejoicing will burst forth from
all sides."

11 - 3 - 35

Sri Aurobindo says:

" Openness in work means
the same thing as openness in
the consciousness. "

12.3.35.

Here Sri Aurobindo answers to your
question:

"The same Force that works in your
consciousness in meditation and clears
away the cloud and confusion whenever
you open to it, can also take up your
action and not only make you aware
of the defects in it but keep you
conscious of what is to be done and
guide your mind and hands to
do it. If you open to it in your
work, you will begin to feel this
guidance more and more until
behind all your activities you will
be aware of the Force of the Mother."

13 - 3 - 35.

(Meditation)

"To turn towards Thee, unite
with Thee, live in Thee and
for Thee, is supreme happiness,
unmixed joy, immutable peace;
it is to breath infinity, to
soar in eternity, no longer
feel one's limits, escape
from time and space."

14 - 3 . 35

Sri Aurobindo says :

" Faithfulness is to admit and to
manifest no other movements but
only the movements prompted
and guided by the Divine."

15 . 3 . 35

(Meditation)

"O Love, resplendent Love, Thou penetratest, Thou transfigurest all."

16 - 3 . 35 .

Aswaghosha has said:

" In the true nature of Matter is
the fundamental law of the Spirit.
In the true nature of Spirit
is the fundamental law of
Matter. "

17 . 3 . 35

(meditation)

"O, the divine splendour of Thy Eternal
Unity!
O, the infinite sweetness of Thy Beatitude.
O, the sovereign majesty of Thy Knowledge!
Thou art the Inconcievable, the Marvellous!"

18 - 3 . 35.

Thales has said:

"Wherever you find movement,
there you find life and a soul."

19 - 3 . 35.

(Meditation)

A new light shall break upon the earth

A new world shall be born.

And the things that were announced

shall be fulfilled. "

20 - 3 - 35.

Asway osha has said:

"Things in their fundamental
nature can neither be named
nor explained. They cannot
be expressed adequately in any
form of language."

21 - 3 - 35.

The Book of Golden Precepts says:

"Flee the Ignorance and flee also the Illusion. Turn thy face from the deceptions of the world; distrust thy senses, they are liars."

22-3-35

(a prayer)

" Accomplish this supreme miracle
so eagerly awaited which will
break down all ignorant egoisms;
awaken Thy sublime flame in
every heart."

23 . 3 - 35.

Lao - Tse has said:

"Something beyond our power
of discrimination existed before
Heaven and Earth. How profound
is its calm! How absolute its
immateriality! It alone exists
and does not change; It
penetrates all and It does not
perish. It may be regarded
as the Mother of the universe.
For myself I know not Its name,
but to give it a name I call
It Tao."

24 . 3 . 35 .

Sri Aurobindo says :

"Sincerity means to lift all the
movements of the being to the level
of the highest consciousness and
realisation already attained

Sincerity exacts the unification
and harmonisation of the whole
being in all its parts and movements
around the central Divine Will."

25.3.35.

Seneca has said:

"We must choose a virtuous man to be always present to our spirit and must live as if we were continually under his eyes and he were scrutinising all that we do."

26 . 3 - 35.

(meditation)

"Lord, Thou hast given me
the happiness infinite, what
being, what circumstance can
have the power to take it away
from me ? "

27 . 3 . 35

The Zohar says:

" It is truly the supreme light,
inaccessible and unknowable,
from which all other lamps
receive their flame and their
splendour."

28.3.35

St Paul has said:

"Therefore thou art inexcusable, O man
whosoever thou art that judgest: for
wherein thou judgest another, thou
condemnest thyself; for thou that
judgest doest the same things."

29 - 3. 35.

(Meditation
    written in October 1914.)

"O Divine Mother, the obstacles shall
be surmounted,
    the enemies appeased,
    Thou shalt dominate the whole
earth with Thy sovereign love,
    and the consciousness of all
shall be illumined with
Thy serenity,
    This is the promise."

30 - 3 - 35.

Baha-Ullah has said:

"In each thing there is a door to
knowledge and in each atom is seen
the trace of the sun."

31 - 3. 35

(Meditation)

"And for a moment, the Master
and the instrument were but
one : the Unique, the Eternal,
The Infinite."

1 . 4 . 35

Hermes has said in adoration:

"O Inexpressible, Ineffable, whom
silence alone can name!"

2 . 4 . 35 .

(a prayer)

O my sweet Master, grant
to all the sovereign benefit
of Thy Illumination ! "

3-4-35.

We read in the Ecclesiasticus:

"My son, if thou hearkenest to me with
application thou shalt be instructed and
if thou appliest thy mind thou shalt
get wisdom."

4 - 4 - 35.

Hermes has said:

"Opinions on the world
and on God are many and
conflicting and I know
not the truth. Enlighten
me, O. my Master."

5 - 4 - 35.

again Hermes has said:

" To be ignorant of the path one
has to take and set out on
the way without a guide,
is to will to lose oneself and
run the risk of perishing."

6 - 4 - 35.

(a prayer)

"Lord, everywhere Thy enemies
appear triumphant; falsehood
is the monarch of the world....
Doubt has usurped the place
of Hope and revolt has pushed
out surrender, Faith is spent,
Gratitude is not born..... -
Lord wilt Thou permit Thy
enemies to prevail, falsehood
and ugliness and suffering to
triumph!"

7-4-35

Patanjali has said:

"The obstacles met by the seeker after concentration are illness, languor, doubt, negligence, idleness, the domination of the senses, false perception, impotence to attain and instability in a state of meditation once attained, ...
Such difficulties are root and product of both physical and mental workings."

8 - 4 . 35

"Alas, O sublime Mother,
how great must be Thy
patience!"

(Written in November 1914 and
still true ...)

9 - 4 - 35

"True surrender enlarges you; it
increases your capacity; it gives
you a greater measure in quality
and in quantity, which you could
not have had by yourself."

10-4-35

St. Paul has said:

" Examine all things and hold
fast that which is good."

11 - 4 - 35.

"The yogi knows by his capacity
for a containing or dynamic identity
with things and persons and
forces."

12 - 4 - 35.

Pascal has said:

"The whole dignity of man
is in thought. Labour then
to think aright."

13 - 4 - 35.

"The movement that stores up
and concentrates is no less needed
than the movement that spreads
and diffuses."

14 - 4 - 35.

"O Lord, Thy sweetness has entered into my soul, and Thou hast filled all my being with joy."

15 - 4 - 35

Marcus Aurelius has said:

"O my soul, wilt thou be one
day simple, one, bare, more visible
than the body which envelops
thee?"

16 - 4 - 35.

" If you ask from within
for peace, it will come."

17-4-35

In the Bhagavad Gita we read:

"The mind is restless, violent, powerful, obstinate; its control seems to me as difficult a task as to control the wind."

18 - 4 - 35.

Ramakrishna has said:

"So long as the mentality
is inconstant and inconsequent,
it is worthless, though one have
a good teacher and the company
of holy men."

19 - 4 . 35 .

The Dhammapada says :

" On his mind vacillating, mobile,
difficult to hold in, difficult to
master. The intelligent man
should impose the same straightness
as an arrow-maker gives to
an arrow. "

20 - 4 - 35

Antoine the Healer has said:

"When a thought rises in us,
let us see whether it is not in
touch with the inferior worlds."

21 . 4 . 35 .

The Mahabharata says :

" By dominating the senses one
increases the intelligence."

22. 4. 35

The Book of Golden
Precepts says:
" Action like inaction may
find its place in thee; if thy
body is in movement, let
thy mind be calm, let thy
soul be as limpid as a
mountain lake."

23 . 4 . 35 .

Chwang-Tse has said:

"When water is still, it reflects objects like a mirror. This stillness, this perfect level is the model of the sage .. The heart of the sage in perfect repose is the mirror of earth and heaven and all existences."

24 - 4 - 35.

Ramakrishna has said:

"The Eternal is seen when
the mind is at rest. When
the sea of the mind is
troubled by the winds of
desire, it cannot reflect
the Eternal and all divine
vision is impossible."

25 - 4 - 35

Ramakrishna has said also:

" So long as a man cries aloud, O Allah, O Allah, be sure he has not yet found his Allah; for whoever has found Him becomes calm and full of peace."

26-4-35.

Carlyle says . . . . .

"Silence, the great empire of silence, loftier than the stars, profounder than the kingdom of death! It alone is great! all the rest is petty."

27 - 4 - 35.

a prayer:

" O Divine Master, Thine is our life, our thought, our love, our whole being. Take possession of Thy own once again ; for Thou art ourselves in our Reality."

28 - 4 - 35.
(meditation)

"In the depths of all that is,
of all that shall be, is Thy
divine and unvarying smile."

29 - 4 - 35

(written on 15-1-33)

Here, each one represents an impossibility to be solved; but as for Thy Divine Grace all is possible, will not Thy Work be, in the detail as in the whole, the accomplishment of all these impossibilities transformed into Divine Realisations."

30 - 4 - 35.

This book closes with the
end of the month. Let it
be also the end of all your
difficulties and troubles,
and the beginning of an
always-happy life.

With love and blessings,